"Edward Carson makes one want to write an essay about the genius of poetry. It would admire his poems' pursuit of self-discovery, their own identities as fictions. It would remark how they try to grasp the present world (the world of online and AI and digital obfuscation) in all its *impresence* and pare it down to its metaphoric minimums. But then it would want to insist that, in the end, all of *twofold* is about metaphor, all metaphors being twofold by definition. It would celebrate the challenge of his work – in his method as much as in his subject matter – of holding two thoughts at once, which is both impossible and manifestly achieved in the poem's own terms. It would note how threads of thought come near without joining, swirl around and away from one another. But the essay would exhaust itself trying to keep up, and in the end the poems would dance circles around it."

Jeffery Donaldson, author of *Missing Link* and *Granted: Poems of Metaphor*

"Wonderfully intriguing, echoic, and fun. With pared-down pairing and whetted wit, Edward Carson's *twofold* tiptoes through the twos, crosses and recrosses that ancient border between mischief and wisdom. An agile bicameral ballet."

Don McKay, author of *Strike/Slip* and *Lurch*

"The poems of *twofold* are constructed on a bedrock of two and three-beat lines and from this simple foundation Carson creates a fantastical architecture of music and metaphor. This edifice is cantilevered so each floor seems to float free from the one below. It is like walking daily past your favorite building and being amazed again by its cornerstone and its crenellations."

Ross Leckie, author of *The Critique of Pure Reason* and *Gravity's Plumb Line*

THE HUGH MacLENNAN POETRY SERIES

Editors: Allan Hepburn and Carolyn Smart

Recent titles in the series

t w o *fold*
fold t w o
2 w o *fold*
fold 2 w o

=

E D W A R D

C A R S O N

McGill-Queen's University Press
Montreal & Kingston • London • Chicago

ISBN 978-0-2280-2009-7 (paper)
ISBN 978-0-2280-2010-3 (ePDF)
ISBN 978-0-2280-2011-0 (ePUB)

Legal deposit second quarter 2024
Bibliothèque nationale du Québec

Printed in Canada on acid-free paper that is 100% ancient forest free
(100% post-consumer recycled), processed chlorine free

Funded by the Government of Canada   Financé par le gouvernement du Canada   Canada   Conseil des arts du Canada   Canada Council for the Arts

We acknowledge the support of the Canada Council for the Arts.

Nous remercions le Conseil des arts du Canada de son soutien.

McGill-Queen's University Press in Montreal is on land which long
served as a site of meeting and exchange amongst Indigenous Peoples,
including the Haudenosaunee and Anishinabeg nations. In Kingston
it is situated on the territory of the Haudenosaunee and Anishinaabek.
We acknowledge and thank the diverse Indigenous Peoples whose
footsteps have marked these territories on which peoples of the world
now gather.

Library and Archives Canada Cataloguing in Publication

Title: Twofold / Edward Carson.

Names: Carson, Edward, 1948- author.

Series: Hugh MacLennan poetry series.

Description: Series statement: The Hugh MacLennan poetry series

Identifiers: Canadiana (print) 20230570844 | Canadiana (ebook)
20230570852 | ISBN 9780228020097 (softcover) |
ISBN 9780228020103 (PDF) | ISBN 9780228020110 (ePUB)

Classification: LCC PS8555.A7724 T86 2024 | DDC C811/.54—dc23

This book was typeset by Marquis Interscript in 9.5/13 Sabon.

for Laura & Matt, Mark & Lindsay

diptych

from Latin *diptycha*, late Greek δίπτυχα

δι- "two/twice" / πτυχή "fold"

A hinged, two-leaved tablet connecting linked objects.

Artwork of two painted or carved panels often
complementing each other and comprising a distinct work
of art from the individual parts.

Short poems: be brief and tell us everything
Charles Simic

The diptych, you see, is beautiful. It is symmetry and difference,
doubling and mirroring, binarism and seriality. It is finite
iteration and open-ended repetition, with or without variation.
It is the form of paradox, both open and closed,
free and contained.
Caroline Bem

CONTENTS

dialogues 1

d i a l o g u e s

to speak between: from Greek *dia* "across, between"
+ *legein* "to speak" from PIE root *leg-* "to gather,"
with derivatives meaning to speak, to pick out words

conversation, discussion between two groups

spoken lines in a dramatic performance

Two birds. One calling. One giving the answer.
Madhur Anand

Rhyme is a bit like metaphor,
a way of asserting a resemblance between otherwise
distant terms.
Kamran Javadizadeh

all dialogue

is a slippery
fish skittish
mischievous

sliding away
as if fleeing

upstream or
maybe down

to a place
on the one hand

of more arrival
than destination

and on the other

to the space shared

between things
one on one
caught in
the arms of
a net longing

to be apprehended

in a poem's

cut and
paste where

beginning
is a virtual
conversion of

someone into

something
else entirely

Ovid knew
to sing
is elemental

confounding

lovers between
each breath

spinning out
continuously
in forests of

reverie and
lamentations

it must be
difficult to
be a poem

being of two
minds words

whirl whistle

like birds
migrating
calling out

with uncertain
expectations

the poem

swoops back
and forth
the way

a thought
fills a breath

singing into it

these words
filling the poem

while last to

speak by half
this echo's

voice repeats
an incomplete

translation
doubling in

the listener
this hunt of

transformation
and paired
configuration

so listen listen

listen to
this ricochet

of words
haunting

the air like
the sorrows
of another world

REPLICATION

where angle
of incidence

meets line
of inclination

love of self
looks long

into the pond
and yet
the more

one stares

the harder it
is to love

this beauty

full of light
burns the eyes
and likeness

is undertow
of binary

and elasticity
of longing

this voice
among voices

being part
borrow and

shadow

where memory
is not the same
as remembering

is division

set adrift
in thickets
of wanting

playing havoc
with reiteration
from another

the scale and
degree of each

part restlessly

splitting love
into fractions

ENTANGLING

where a voice
roams nearby

roads diverge

direction is
difficult and

conversation
a struggle yet

when a lover

speaking words
snared in
lonely fields

hears another

responding
in riddles
of dispersal

a physics
of concentration
reckons it's

really a rounding
error of belief

circumnavigating
a geometry
of the poem

all elements

held inside
are vessels
of containment

whereas

when the less
of limitation
makes more

is language
renewed in

the mirrors
of metaphor

its concentric
limits caught

in the wake

of multiplying
outcomes

this vanity
of poetry
probing

a vision
of itself

swarms into
the anything

but sheltered
forest

of the page

yet the page

has its own
agenda as a

field of fluid
reflections

peopled by
creatures of
circumstance

briefly thought
to be immutable

COUNTERPOINT

the sylvan
voice rides
a breeze

within this
full moon's

radiance
of promise

while later
when rhymes

in the wood
mitigate

and stretch
no further

all argument
finds common
purpose with

each word

assuming
the emphasis

of startled leaves

COUNTERBALANCE

red shakes
as maple

wakes buds

breaking free
in barking

wind of stir
and churn

while clarity
of crimson
fruit is

counterweight

of cause and
consequence

all branches
resisting

love's opposite

to be reckoned
with when

red will shake

CANTILEVERED

in a world

of one lover
reaching out
to another

where simple
is seldom

linear
yet commonly
circumspect

a poem juts

into space

its musing a
delicate timing

in brink
and float

and offset
of meaning
in a story

of gravity
denied

BONSAI

in miniature
a kind of
slow evolving

familiarity
this twin

and echo
of another
matches and

modifies by
twist or snip

though left
to its own
devices

evolution
swaps
subtraction

for addition
exaggerating
out of all

proportion
prophetic needles
frail in hyperbole

DILEMMA

a lover's needs
struggle with
the choices

of one and
not the other

the obstacle
a problematic

unbreakable

circumference

being that part
of ourselves

that can't be
unravelled or

undone or like
the closed loops

we make tying
things together

an arrangement
all too easily
open to knots

rising slowly
in the time

of now you
see it now
you don't

a liaison
with obstacles

is potent

incongruity
of one lover
with another

its entropy of

emotions
a crackling

phosphorescence

relinquishing
deliberation to
a clockwork of

incoherence at
a higher speed

DESTINATION

its soft stroke
out of reach

amoureuse

is sympathetic
air kiss

or nudge
circumscribed

from lip
to cheek

getting around
the question

and unsolved
reckoning of

where all this
might end up

sex is already
ridiculous

so where else
to travel to
but in between

ORIGAMI

calling out
this lover's
contretemps

is summons
and dismiss

though also
metaphor

folding time

or could it
be a poetry
transparently

misleading

its narrative
a furrowed
argument

of love lost
yet continuing

its misadventure

of dispute in
papery contortions

DENOTATION

when all
is said
and done

because
of the way
wind and

tree bend in

the presence
of mass and

energy
the flexibility

of love
is at times
a literal

articulation

of opposites

everywhere
a likeness

reluctantly
unrecognizable

CONNOTATION

like water
beading

on glass

this arching
attention to
the surface

tension

of lovers
having both

an invocation
and individual
momentum

is the physics
of flotation

and sidelong
adhesion

of push pull

with intervals
of internal
surrender

most adored

some say to
be loved is
a shape with

the inclination
of a curve

or some kind
of murmur like

a craquelure
of intimations

most beloved

there is some
suspicion now

this contour
of affection
can't be

shared as
all angles

point in other
directions

CATARACT

all vanity

is direction
so capricious

it slips and
flows across
all networks

of temptation

cascades
and tumbles

headlong to
indulgence
but often ends

in escalation
of equivocation

its indifference

to exception
and deception

pools infatuation
of design with
irresistible force

SOLENOID

when lovers
are positive
and negative

it's simile

of separate
parts in fields

true with
others less

like minded

not unlike
scarlet and

flaxen leaves
at some point

coiling into
flame

or the lure
of a poem

circling through
electric lines of
plus and minus

MAGNETISM

in the arms
of the page

the poem
is persuasive

its pathways
asymmetrical
crossroads

of attraction
and resistance

but it lingers
in place only

to be released

by the mind

a magnitude
of endlessness

where it soars
and untangles

cuts this close
only to travel
a great distance

reliability
strays with
unruly eyes

as fidelity

at least from
an acute angle

often bends
inward

into error

when the
further we
look away

from one
to another

a diagonal

of displacement
defeats us

a tangential
trick we never
see coming

GLITCH

in songs
of the heart

a fitful snag
is interest

interrupted

unexpected
but restless

nevertheless

a short lived
digression
from attention

but commonly
self correcting

this mere
of diversion
is an affair

of the self
and collision of

intention turning
unintentional

ASSIGNATION

every page

consents to
the poem's
corresponding

soft embrace

every word
embodying

a choreography
of correlatives

though each
line is both
parenthesis

and rendezvous

reciprocally
algorithmic

the quantum
of which is

a fluency of
parallel
approximations

says a lover
to another

as emotions
unfold

prime's a
whole number
plus encounter

with the other
while composite

is combination
of expressions

though being
desired is not

the same as

feeling desired
a dichotomy

of opposites
alternating

into pleasures
most infinite

like metaphor
with a lover
at its centre

this whirligig

of roundabout
continuous

momentum

teases out
spin with

zero torque
velocities

of circular
consistency

while finding
attitude of axis

tantalizes with
pitch or plunge

and performance
is a feeling
ambidextrous

passionately

promotional
and clearly
emotional

this twofold
online
sophistry

is resonance
in a rhyming

history ever
so discreetly

susceptible
to peripheral

mysteries
where seduction

in expression

is angular
momentum

of electrons
most promiscuous

GILT

skin deep
this media
lately

in mind

is a lighter
leaner love
of checks

passing by

like minded
balances

a lover asks

between
substance
and surface

might this be

the voice of
metaphysics or
according to

interpretations
truth in motion

daytime
simmers

into night
while night
ices day

or is it regret

looking to be
the veneer
of conscience

its conspiracy

a thinly
applied coat

of character
on top of

a morally
close knit

scruple of

meticulous
tight lipped
collusion

allegory

will mostly
reveal itself

the betrayal
of this or
the that of

was or soon
to be sings
to another

of dichotomy

pries open
a drama of

cause or
duality
of effect

asks not
the wherefore

of countless

modifications
but why not

when lovers
slide side
to side in

performance
oh so firmly

pertinacious

the one and
none of
disposition

arches
centripetally

each inflection
pleasurably

concave

inexplicitly

centrifugal
and convex

its path of
binary bend
mostly operatic

one needs to

ask if a body
of language

turning into
another shape
is more than

itself then how

to measure
such evolution

if metamorphosis
that strays is
also contained

in changes made

as if each shift
were a trial and

error of value
or echo of myth
in conjuring

one thing from
parts of another

like language
updating itself

it's unspeakable

to summarize
then historize

the DNA of
renewing or
restoring an

unresolved love

yet to recombine
then redesign

by means of
proxy is likely

where data
is hybrid rhyme
with a twist

such possibility
an analogy to

cloning similarity
with a difference

mindful
of possibility

in the power
of plea

special care
is needed in

asking to
be loved

each reply

bristling
like a number

divisible
by itself

with a theory
of its own

where forests
of words

hide heartache
invisible with
voice reprised

GHOST

arriving
afterwards

grief enters
the present
to summon

a prickling
apprehension

its emptying
a suspension

taking flight
radically

dispersing in
one direction

dissolving
in another

this whirling
of an unearthly

voice enfolding

an exhaustion
of the light

CHATTER

what's   said
                    sotto voce
so chattily

                    dispatched
    tattling of one

                    trifling another
withholding

    nothing too

                    personal in
the face of
            all intended

    revelations
                    is perplexing

all the same
            this being

            the half truth
    of a whole

                    with a lot
left over

            in between

b i n a r i e s

binary
from the Late Latin *binarius* "two together"
bini- "twofold" / *bis* "double" / PIE root duo- "two"
a computer coding system using the binary digits 0 and 1
a form consisting of two interrelated parts

Where two convene, a third is always present.
Karen Solie

APOLOGIA

with Homer
                all narrative

twists and turns
                in a kind of

                contrapposto
of curve and
                counterweight

        it's enough to

compound reality
                or ordinary

                        thought
but any explanation

                one moment
    to the next
                is fluid enough

its arguments
                caught in

the wake of
                velocity fields

        of infinite choice

this number so
conspicuous not

always where
it seems to be
is much ado

about nothing

being neither
the quantum of
minus or plus

nor vessels
of love or loss
yet nothing is

as singular
or sweetly

so dissimilar

as is this sly
practitioner of

eloquent infinity

and slipstream of
unbroken thought

this lover
of the other
inseparable

yet separate
where gender
as you like it

adds up when
partners tally

in this drama

what's true of
one and none

is both disguise
and counterpart

met together

breathing in
all numbers

with blush
of binary

and splash
of in between

cutting across
the internet

poetry cruises

in a kind of
Möbius ship

between a
zero and one
with two

sides of two
edges tied in

twist and turn

its readers
seeking out
searchable

virtual shores
of longing

and mystery

sung to in
the wake of
another's tongue

will this be
loved once
like a lover

or last left
once loved

and yet at
first light
this story

forsaking
belief is

information
jostled about

transforming

a likeness
of dual
sense

its shadow

seeming more
accomplice

than complicity

HEADS

love knows

where the
poem goes

hoping
to speak
to one who

seeks out
words so

playfully
abuzz

it follows
a physics

of air borne
heads and tails

falling
headlong in

to the mind's
infatuation
with quantum

flirtations

if you look
close enough

at the angle
from which

it sallies forth

all signs are
it's geometry

of journey

or might it
be a signature
of lovers

and aftermath
of tumbling

particles
at play

randomly
moving to
where letting

loose is what
entangles all

with a *whirr*
and glow of
the screen

pixels sail
into emptiness

wind blown

in one to
one ratios

a wooing

portrait
of data

swarming in
the beholder's .
eye this

crisscrossing

of 0s and 1s
mimicking

murmurations
chasing light
into every face

MARRIAGE

when zero

is wedded
with one
the logical

longitude
of lovers at

the far flung
outskirts of

everything
numerical

begins to
feel like
geography

is interactive
and measure

for measure
personal space

looks to create

somewhere
from nothing

FISCAL

of more and

less we sing
in arithmetic

an aesthetic
so artfully
meticulous

yet little

is more
diametric

than when
equations in
the beauty

of a line
circling

the square
are sum and

difference

in the allure
of accumulation
taxed and spent

this longing
for numbers

banking on
a compound
realm of

short or long
supply is

of interest
to no one

but to many
this interest

in interest
is attraction

at a greater
degree when

like seduction

a currency of
interchange

converts obstacle
into possible

natural
language
processing

traversing
the input

from large
language

paradigms

is artificial
intelligence

from deep
learning

algorithms

in the wake
of searches

where hard
problems asked
are easy and

easy problems
are hard

this peripatetic
perambulation

and clamour
for whatness

are song
and response

of 0 and 1

though its
quest for

no nonsense
all in a row

AI fidelity

is a matter
of fact

abcdminded

noise of
numbers

and gesture
of being itself

PROPHESY

a two way
chart in dual

plotted parts
this devotion

to notation
is weather of

rain or shine
a back to front

start to finish
climate of low

to high pressure
and forecast of

now or hereafter
its measure

a foretelling
and atmospheric

embodiment
of variable

disturbances with
lightning in pairs

breathless
is the line

concurrently
dividing and
joining two

points or so
said Euclid

who knew
that heaven
and earth in

figure and
curve contain

a ferocious

certainty of
circumference

beyond which

no boundary
or circumstance

exists to limit
any destination

NETWORK

all lovers

with nothing
in mind

and nowhere
in particular
to go zig

zag through
boundless

coordinates and
hemispheres
of likes

this propensity
alternating

from pillar
to post
is vacillation

right and left

with lopsided
proximities

everywhere

of Euclid
Kafka said

the point to
be reached

is the point
where there
can be no

turning back
whereas

for Euclid

the point is
a converging
thought of

both horizon
and boundary

an axiom that
direction is a

distance best

experienced
from afar

FIDELITY

of beliefs
and binaries

to be lived

we sing of
screen nation

echoing its

stories and
seductive
meanderings

its sorting
of thought

into like
us or not

is politically
adventurous

its nature
asymmetric

with reflections

most isometric .

downstream
of online
politics

all signs point
to emotions

driven by
what isn't

us must be
like a fish

out of water

all passions
and gyrations

gills squeezing
mouth flaring
out syllables

in breathless
declarations

are far too toxic

to accommodate
a second thought

from what
is concealed

all language

travels alive
anxious to
uncover what

is real
and what

has yet to
be revealed

whereupon
a ghostly
truth arrives

as coexistence

of states in
whereabouts
of words turns

quantum

of thought into
superposition

like a lover
with another

connection
and a network

are parts of
each other

their leafy

tendrils and
and boughs
a labyrinth

and message

of theological
proportions

it's whispered
we'll soon be

gods though
the guidelines

are neither
clear nor equally
limited or infinite

some say
the angry

fret and vex
of zero

is jargon
as it spins
heat into

information
or bias into

algorithm yet

its emphasis
is emptiness

an integer
with feelings
of something

foreshadowing
the countless

one and only

enfolding fever
of infinity

evermore
gamely cool
and catchy

the whole
online kit

and caboodle
is so collage

how very
cunning its

collective
yawp and
fractious fume

its singular

seethe of

cross words

at cross
purposes when

all things are
so much easier
said than done

math is
less than
figurative

more like
a metaphor

interrogating
itself in an

odyssey of
hypotheses

or prophesy

adding in
the pairing

of philosophy

where all
data mingles
together as

metaphysics

the nature of
corollary turning
one into many

now that
the internet

is spectacle
turning us
into gods

all perspective
is perplexed

zeroing in
on curves of

famous for
being famous

identity into
impersonation

some say it's
subtraction of
context while

simple division

says it separates
us from seeing

any difference

COMPLICARE

so very
ill equipped
to navigate

what online
is to love

our words

ad lib
wildly adrift

diverging from
common sense

while inflection

folding us
together also

pulls us apart
in cockeyed
cants where

everyone's
concavity

is equally
convex

VIRAL

with a giddy
sideways post

a lover asks

of another
in a twitter
of words

have we set
free the ego

or could it be
we really are
a chemistry

of causality
flying wild

while social
media says

it's irrefutable

when no power
of the tongue

can put down
what's irresistible

ENTANGLEMENT

consider a
coin at rest

its real purpose
heads *or* tails

but tossed
in the air

the physics
of in between
is different

being in flight
neither one *nor*
the other with

the possibility

of both where
two things

sharing space

are quantum
cause to join

close up
or far apart

for Heraclitus

the way up
and way down
add up to

the same story

which boils
down to

connect the
dots quarrels

over less
is more

or the need
to hold parts

apart yet
together like

accounts of
what's settled
or outstanding

as the sum total
of any measure

the idea of
nothing is

an algorithm
of sorts

empty of
the visible
and temporal

with a proof
not delivering

a theorem

but a conjecture
on absence

its intersection

between page
and thought

is a turbulence
in the eddies
of the mind

creasing parallel
tales in two

having bided
its time

it arrived
from far off

each A to Z
became the
arithmetic

of a 0 and 1

while today

there are
new rules to
accommodate

though rule
or be ruled is

the anarchy of
algorithm with

intelligence
artificially

bringing order
to the unruly

BELOVED

on a simple
closed surface

in the plain
conceit of
its dimension

a straight line

setting sail in
one direction

in due time
meets another

resulting in
an unspoken
attraction

and allure

of tentative
proportions

their closeness

manifest but
unable to be
measured

PROPORTION

in preferences
of him or her
and pairings at

cross sections

one might
see obtuse

as not unlike
acute within

ratios of
inclination

their pleasures
being rhymes
of variation

foreseeing
a match at

mid journey

folded into
abbreviation

and clatter
of credibility

a pirouette
so intimate

it weaves its
own geography

the circle is
gyration of

a singular

intensity
while square

is more a
semaphore

of *do-si-do*
and waltz

an equilibrium
cheek-to-cheek

where squaring
the circle
lover to lover

is geometry
two steps apart

if urge
is a circle
interrupted

and voyage

a roundabout

line of reason
the appeal
of desire's

buoyancy
powering
conversion

amounts to
a delicious

cause effect

and devious
assembly

inside a rational
sense of unlike

directions with
unthinkable reach

SIMILAR

not sameness

but more a
pooling of
reflection

and rhyming
redirection

what the eye

interrupted
by deflection

sees together
with the ear
when it hears

what the voice
voices and a

mind perceives

this pleat of
resemblance

like finding
one meaning
inside another

numbers
never meet

but wear
themselves

out trying
to draw near

while hand
in glove

they calibrate
then circulate

in fractions
close to but
never quite

coalescing

what's similar
in one being

sympathetically
tucked into

difference
in another

when nothing's
            left to say

save where in
            all geometry
      something's

always hidden
            in plane sight

it's plain to
            see proficiency

and agility
            in numbers
      passing for

a recipe
            of what we

hope to analyze

or mostly need
            to crystalize

as a poetry
            of things

like no other

Sincere thanks once again to Allan Hepburn and Carolyn Smart for their continuing support, insights, and suggestions. My gratitude also goes out to the many dedicated and professional publishing teams at McGill-Queen's University Press who helped in making the book ready for its readers.

And, as always, to Brian, who understands sometimes there are some things better left unsaid and is always ready to read when reading is the hardest thing to do.

Short poems: be brief and tell us everything, Charles Simic, Notebooks 1996–2006.

The diptych, you see . . . from Caroline Bem, "A Moveable Form: The Diptych in Art, Book Culture, and (Post) Cinema" (PhD diss., McGill University, 2015), 10–11.

Two birds. One calling. One giving the answer. Madhur Anand, "Rising Variance as an Early Warning," *Parasitic Oscillations* (McClelland & Stewart, 2022), 33.

Rhyme is a bit like metaphor . . . Kamran Javadizadeh, "The Eroticism of an Ikea Bed," *The New Yorker*, 3 February 2023.

Where two convene . . . Karen Solie, "The Spies," *The Caiplie Caves* (House of Anansi Press, 2019), 26.

In *"prompt"*: *hard / problems / are easy and / easy problems / are hard*, from Steven Pinker, *The Language Instinct* (Perennial Modern Classics, Harper, 2007), 190.

In "searching": *"abcdminded,"* James Joyce, *Finnegans Wake*.

In "searching": "gestures of being itself," Marshall McLuhan, *James Joyce: Trivial and Quadrivial*, 1953.